BEGINNING HISTORY

Crusaders
Egyptian Pyramids
Greek Cities
Medieval Markets
Norman Castles
Roman Soldiers
Saxon Villages
Tudor Sailors
Victorian Children
Viking Explorers

All words that appear in **bold** are explained in the glossary on page 22.

Series and book editor: Catherine Ellis
Designer: Helen White

First published in 1989 by Wayland (Publishers) Limited,
61 Western Road, Hove, East Sussex, BN3 1JD

British Library Cataloguing in Publication Data
Place, Robin
Saxon villages.
1. Great Britain. Anglo–Saxon settlements
I. Title II. Series
941.01

ISBN 0–85210–817–7

Typeset by Kalligraphics Limited, Horley, Surrey.
Printed in Italy by G. Canale & C.S.p.A., Turin.
Bound in Belgium by Casterman S.A.

CONTENTS

SAXON SETTLERS

The Saxons invaded Britain in the fifth century AD. They came from northern Europe, looking for land to farm. There were many battles between the Britons and the invading Saxons, but by AD 700 most of what is now England was taken over by Saxon settlers.

Each group of Saxon raiders was led by a king, and he divided up a lot of his newly-won land among his **bodyguards**. It was their reward for fighting for him. In turn, these warriors shared out some of this land among their followers.

Most Saxons were farmers. As they settled down, groups of them built villages. There was more forest in England than there is now. The settlers cut down trees to build their big wooden houses.

Saxon settlers felling trees to build farmhouses. The tree trunks were taken to the village site in a cart pulled by oxen.

Many farmers owned slaves who worked for them. Slaves were prisoners captured in war, criminals, or children whose parents had sold them because they were too poor to feed them.

SAXON VILLAGES

The first Saxon villages were built on hill-tops. In time, the Saxons moved down into valleys, where the land grew better crops.

In some villages, houses were built along a long street. In others, houses were grouped together around a village green near a church. Most villages had a stout fence around them to keep out wolves and raiders.

Saxon families – parents, children, grandparents, aunts and uncles and animals – usually all lived in the same house, so it had to be large! A typical house measured about

Above *and* **Below** *Archaeologists have tried to rebuild Saxon huts and workshops to show what they looked like.*

19 metres long and 7 metres wide, and took about 18 big oak trees to build. The walls were made of posts set in a **trench**. In the middle of the house was a big fire.

Saxons had **stables**, **byres** and **granaries**. In the farmyard there were workshops for weaving or making pots, and huts for storage.

A typical Saxon village beside a river.

A Farmer's Crops

In Saxon times, fields were divided into long narrow strips. The farmers' strips of land were scattered to give everyone some good and some poor land. Farmers also had **pasture** for their sheep and cows, and hayfields.

Farmers **cultivated** their fields with ploughs. On heavy soil it took up to eight oxen to pull the plough, so several farmers would share their oxen and take it in turns to use the plough. The long narrow strips of field made ploughing easier, because the farmer did not have to turn the plough very often.

Ploughing and sowing corn. Children had to scare birds away so that they did not gobble up the seed corn.

Corn was harvested with **sickles** and **scythes**, and threshed with wooden **flails**. The grains were then tossed into the air so the wind blew away the **chaff**, then it was carefully stored in granaries. **Flax** was grown to make linen, and blue and red dyes were made from **woad** and **madder**.

FARM ANIMALS

Saxon farmers kept cattle and sheep for their meat and for milk. They made the milk into butter and cheese. They kept pigs, which they drove into the woods every day to feed on acorns and beechmast. Farmers also kept hens and geese for their eggs.

Horses were used to pull wagons and carts, and for riding. Dogs helped the villagers to drive the farm animals to their pastures from their byre. Cats caught the rats and mice that ate the grain and stores of food.

Saxons also kept sheep for their wool. The women spun and wove the wool into cloth. Goat hair was made into blankets to keep the family warm at night, and the hides of goats

Above *A Saxon drawing of a shepherd boy looking after his sheep.*

Below *Farmers threshing corn with flails, to loosen the hard outer case round the grain.*

and cows could be made into shoes, ropes, leather bottles, belts and other things people needed.

Sometimes animals were stolen, but the thieves were severely punished if they were caught.

Men stealing sheep from a village at night.

SAXON WOMEN

Farmers' wives were very busy, but they had their family and slaves to help them. Every day the cows and **ewes** had to be milked. Some milk was made into butter and cheese. There were hens to feed, and their eggs to be collected. The women also had to bake the bread. Saxons made all their own clothes using wool or linen, which they wove on a loom.

In late summer and autumn, women were especially busy, helping with the harvest, and planning ways to store their food. When an animal was killed, some of the meat was smoked or salted so it could be kept for the winter without going bad. If the village was near a river, fish was also smoked or salted.

When the evening meal was finished women sat by the fire. But they still worked, spinning wool into thread while they talked or listened to someone telling a story.

Women working in the farmyard. A girl is carrying wood indoors to keep the fire burning.

SAXON CHILDREN

Village children did not go to school. Almost as soon as they could walk there was work for them to do, either indoors helping their mothers, or out on the farm. Children spent a lot of time collecting wood for the fire in the house, which burned day and night.

In the spring, children had to stop birds eating the grain sown in the fields. They threw stones at them, sometimes using **slings**. Children also drove the geese to graze in grassy fields. They had to watch over them so that foxes and wolves did not carry one off.

The children's favourite time of year was August, when beekeepers

Above *A beekeeper banging on a full skep to drive the bees up into an empty one.*

Below *Men keeping warm by a fire. Collecting firewood was a job for children.*

drove bees out of the woven **skep** into a new one so they could take the **honeycomb**. Sometimes the children would get a little bit of the honeycomb to eat.

Life was quite hard for Saxon children, and many died young from diseases.

A SAXON WATER-MILL

For many years Saxon women had to grind corn into flour using hand-mills. But by the ninth century, the Saxons had started to build water-mills.

Water-mills were built near rivers. A channel was dug between the river and the mill so the water flowed into a millpond. Wooden planks set around the sides of the pond kept the water in.

To work the mill, water was let out of the pond to run over a big **water-wheel**. The running water turned the wheel. Above the water-wheel, on the floor of the mill, there were two big **millstones** placed one on top of the

Above *Milling flour was dusty work. When the millers were thirsty they drank ale from a pitcher like this.*

Right *Some old millstones. They were made from hard rock so that bits of stone did not get mixed with the flour.*

other. The water-wheel was joined to the upper millstone by a **shaft**. As the wheel went round, the millstone turned. The miller poured grain between the stones, and they ground the grain into flour.

A water-mill with part of the walls and floor cut away to show how it worked.

A SAXON CHURCH

The first Saxon settlers believed in many gods. In AD 597 they began to learn about Christianity and to build churches.

At first, churches were built of wood. In later years, bigger churches were built of stone. The church had two parts. The **nave** was where people stood to hear the services. It had an earth floor, and there were no pews to sit on. Babies were baptized in a stone **font**. At the east end of the nave was an arch leading to the **chancel** and the altar, where the priest stood.

The church had a tower, with a bell that was rung when it was time for a service. It had a thick wooden door with an iron lock. Church windows were small, so it was dark inside and had to be lit by candles. Few Saxon churches had stained-glass windows, but wooden **shutters** kept the rain out. People were buried in the churchyard.

Building a new stone church. Men are making mortar in a sort of Saxon concrete mixer.

Villagers at a feast, listening to a man singing and playing the harp.

AMUSEMENTS

After work, villagers liked to tell stories by firelight, to sing, and play board games with dice and bone counters. They made up **riddles** about everyday things, making them so strange that friends could not guess the answer. For example, Question: what creature has two ears, one eye, two feet and twelve hundred heads? Answer: a one-eyed man selling heads of garlic.

At certain times of the year, such as at ploughing and harvest time, the Saxons had feasts. At these feasts, a small **harp** was passed around. Everyone was expected to sing to it in turn, making up verses.

Sometimes travellers came to the village: **jugglers**, **pedlars**, men bringing a bull or bear to be **baited** by dogs, or one of the king's messengers. They were welcomed because they brought news of what was happening outside the village.

A drawing from a Saxon book, of musicians playing.

GLOSSARY

Bear and Bull Baiting A cruel sport in which dogs were made to attack an animal.

Bodyguards Men who protected the king.

Byre A shelter used for animals.

Chaff The hard husk around a grain of corn.

Chancel The east end of a church.

Cultivate To make land ready for growing crops.

Ewe A female sheep.

Flail A piece of wood that swings loosely from a handle, used as a tool for beating grain.

Flax A plant whose stems can be made into linen.

Font A stone basin in a church, holding holy water for baptisms.

Granary A farm building where grain is stored.

Harp A wooden musical instrument, with strings that are plucked to make music.

Honeycomb A mass of wax cells made by bees to store their honey.

Juggler An entertainer who throws up and catches several balls at once. Saxons also juggled with knives.

Madder A plant from whose roots a red dye is made.

Millstone A thick round stone used to grind corn in a mill. It had to be of very hard rock so that bits of stone did not get mixed with the flour.

Nave The west end of a church.

Pasture Grassy fields where animals graze.

Pedlars People who went from village to village selling their goods.

Riddle A puzzling question.

Scythe A curved iron blade on the end of a long handle, used for mowing.

Shaft A long wooden pole.

Shutters Pieces of wood put across a window to keep out rain, often used before there were glass windows.

Sickle A curved iron blade on a short handle, used for cutting corn.

Skep A round basket used as a beehive.

Sling A length of string with a piece of leather in the middle to hold a stone. With a sling, stones can be hurled further than by throwing them.

Stable A building for horses.

Trench A deep ditch.

Water-wheel A wooden wheel with flaps or paddles, that is turned by running water.

Woad A tall plant with yellow flowers from which a blue dye is made.

Books To Read

A Saxon Farmer by Stewart Ross (Wayland, 1985)

Alfred the Great and the Saxons by Robin May (Wayland, 1984)

The Anglo-Saxon Household by Jean Ellenby (CUP, 1986)

The Saxons by Tony D. Triggs (Macdonald, 1979)

The Saxons by Barry and Anne Steel (Wayland, 1985)

Saxon Britain by Tony D. Triggs (Wayland, 1989)

INDEX

Picture Acknowledgements

The publisher would like to thank the following for supplying the photographs in this book: Aldus Archive 10 (both), 14 (bottom), 21; Michael Holford 16 (top); The National Trust Photographic Library (Mike Williams) 16 (bottom); Mr Tutton 14 (top); The Weald and Downland Open Air Museum 6 (top); The West Stow Anglo-Saxon Village Trust 6 (bottom).